Roman Soldier

School Girl

W9-CED-101

Roller Blades

Mechanic

Doctor

African Musician

Mom

Dad

Brother

Sister

Grandma   # Grandad

Skateboarder

Greek Scholar

Baby

Judge

Greek Soldier

Victorian Lady

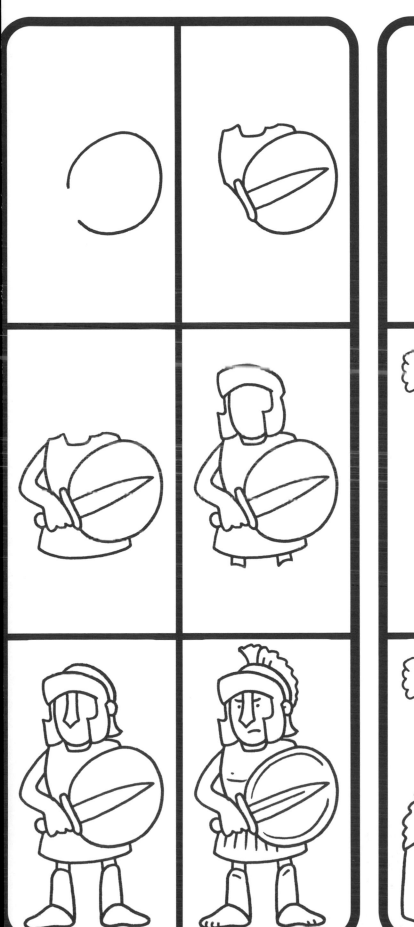

Teddy Boy

Teacher

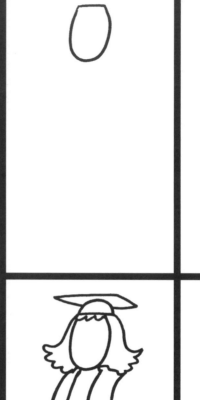

Black Belt

Sailor

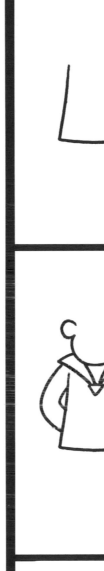

Tennis Player

Builder

Roman Emperor   Nurse

Diver

Burglar

Dentist

Soccer Player

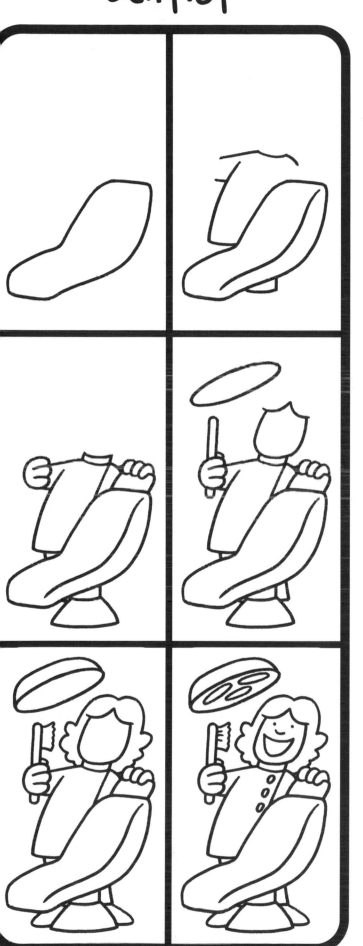

Chef

Elf

Gardener

Baseball Player

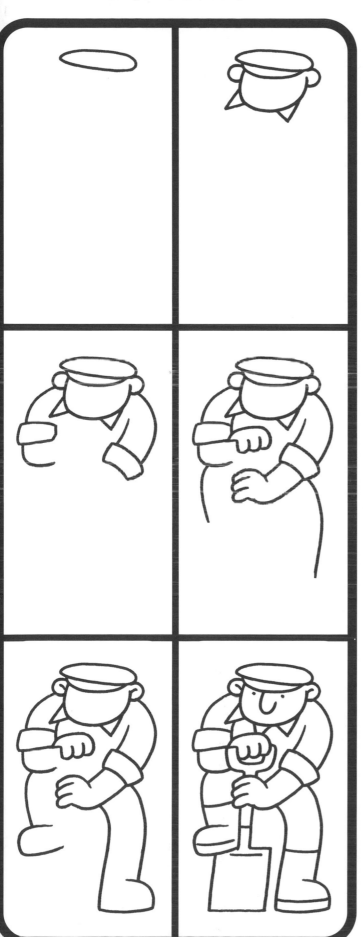

Tightrope Walker

Fisherman

Policeman

Mailman

Eskimo   Scuba Diver

Victorian Gentleman

Ballet Dancer

Viking   Jump

Actor

Handstand

Deep Sea Diver

Wizard

Captain